BODY

Contents

Your amazing body!

Your body is like an amazing, complicated machine. Lots of different parts work closely together to make it possible for you to live and grow.

Your brain is the control center!

As you breathe, you take in oxygen, needed by all parts of the body.

Your digestive system takes food and turns it into energy.

Muscles are responsible for every movement you make.

4

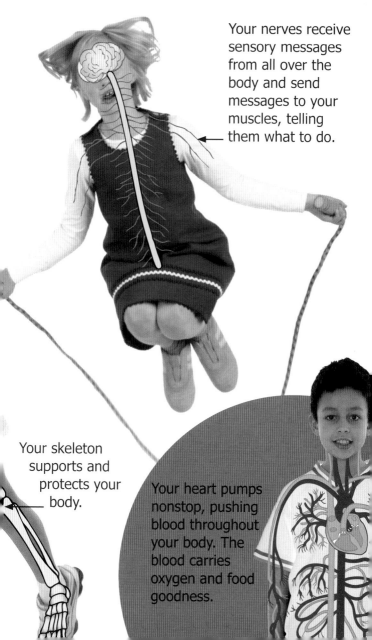

Your nerves receive sensory messages from all over the body and send messages to your muscles, telling them what to do.

Your skeleton supports and protects your body.

Your heart pumps nonstop, pushing blood throughout your body. The blood carries oxygen and food goodness.

Your skeleton

More than 200 bones fit together
to form your skeleton. This
frame gives your body strength
and protects the soft parts
inside. Without a skeleton,
you could not stand.

Your ribs form a cage
that protects your
heart and lungs.

A joint is where two bones meet. Your thigh
bone fits into your pelvis at your hip joint.

Did you know?

Together, your two hands contain
more than one-quarter of the bones
in your body!

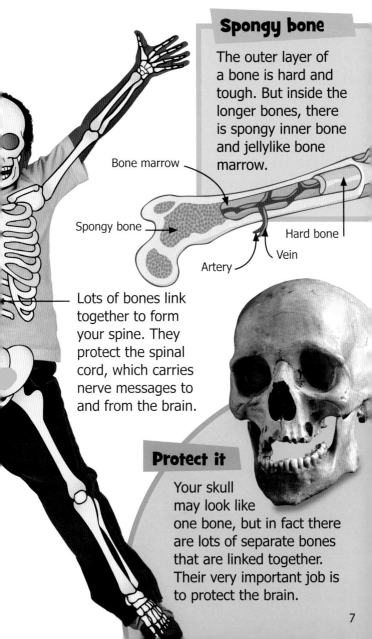

Spongy bone

The outer layer of a bone is hard and tough. But inside the longer bones, there is spongy inner bone and jellylike bone marrow.

Bone marrow

Spongy bone

Artery

Vein

Hard bone

Lots of bones link together to form your spine. They protect the spinal cord, which carries nerve messages to and from the brain.

Protect it

Your skull may look like one bone, but in fact there are lots of separate bones that are linked together. Their very important job is to protect the brain.

7

Muscles

There are about 650 muscles in your body, mostly attached to bones. Every movement you make depends on muscles. You use about 200 different muscles just walking!

Chest muscles help you to breathe. —

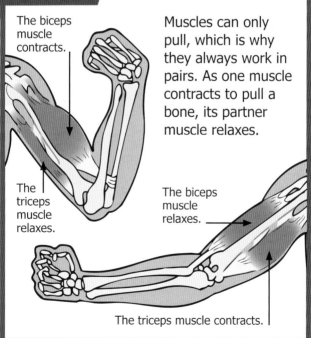

The biceps muscle contracts.

Muscles can only pull, which is why they always work in pairs. As one muscle contracts to pull a bone, its partner muscle relaxes.

The triceps muscle relaxes.

The biceps muscle relaxes. —

The triceps muscle contracts.

8

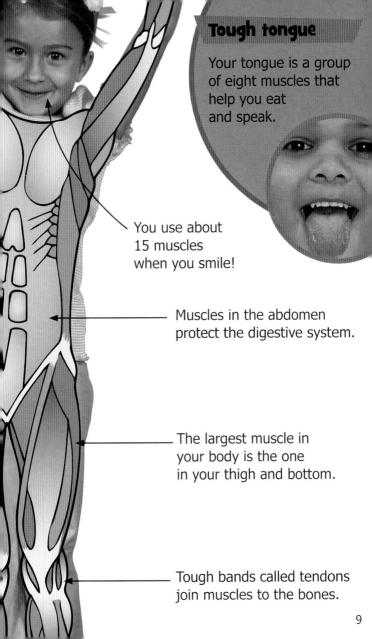

Tough tongue

Your tongue is a group of eight muscles that help you eat and speak.

You use about 15 muscles when you smile!

Muscles in the abdomen protect the digestive system.

The largest muscle in your body is the one in your thigh and bottom.

Tough bands called tendons join muscles to the bones.

9

Your heart is a very strong muscle that works nonstop. It pumps blood all around your body. The blood carries oxygen and food to keep your body working. Your heart is so strong that it only takes a minute to pump blood to your toes and back again!

Veins carry blood back towards the heart.

Arteries take blood away from the heart.

Blood

Blood is made up of red blood cells, white blood cells, and platelets in a liquid called plasma. Red blood cells carry oxygen around the body. White blood cells fight germs.

Red blood cell

White blood cell

Germ

Plasma

If you get cut, platelets help the blood to clot. The blood also carries food to the cells.

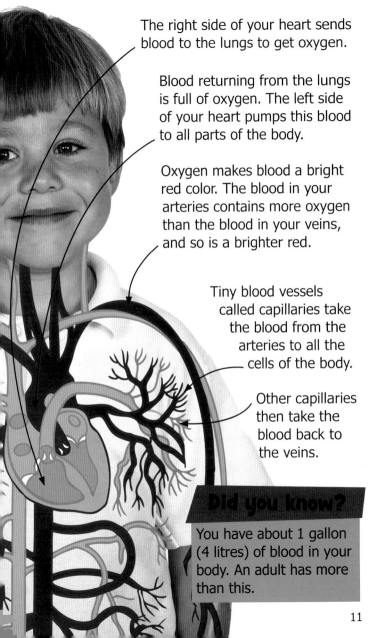

The right side of your heart sends blood to the lungs to get oxygen.

Blood returning from the lungs is full of oxygen. The left side of your heart pumps this blood to all parts of the body.

Oxygen makes blood a bright red color. The blood in your arteries contains more oxygen than the blood in your veins, and so is a brighter red.

Tiny blood vessels called capillaries take the blood from the arteries to all the cells of the body.

Other capillaries then take the blood back to the veins.

Did you know?

You have about 1 gallon (4 litres) of blood in your body. An adult has more than this.

11

Breathing

We have to breathe all the time to stay alive. When we breathe, our lungs absorb oxygen from the air and pass carbon dioxide out into the air.

Muscles between the ribs contract and move the ribs out to pull air into the lungs.

The diaphragm is a big sheet of muscle. It contracts and moves down as you breathe in.

A big shout!

You can use the air passing in and out of your lungs to make noises. The voice box contains flaps, called vocal cords, which vibrate as the air goes through. Muscles control what sound the vocal cords make.

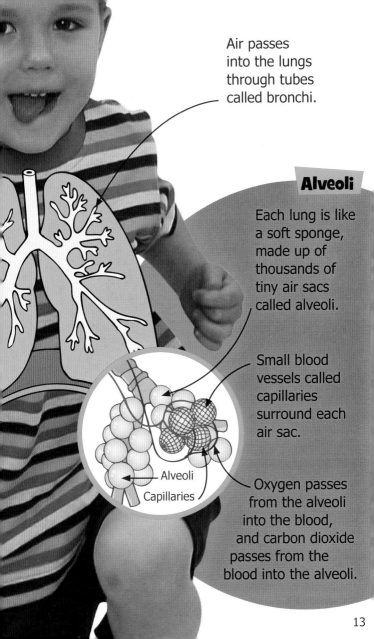

Air passes into the lungs through tubes called bronchi.

Alveoli

Each lung is like a soft sponge, made up of thousands of tiny air sacs called alveoli.

Small blood vessels called capillaries surround each air sac.

Alveoli

Capillaries

Oxygen passes from the alveoli into the blood, and carbon dioxide passes from the blood into the alveoli.

Eating

You eat to provide your body with fuel, so that it can grow, keep itself healthy, and have plenty of energy. The digestive system is like a long tube, running from your mouth to your bottom. As food passes along the different parts of the tube, it is gradually broken up, broken down, and absorbed.

Liver _____

Goodness and waste

Your liver receives blood full of goodness from the food you have eaten. It stores some things and changes what is not wanted into waste. When your kidneys filter the blood, they remove this waste liquid and pass it to your bladder.

Kidney

Your bladder stores waste water. _____

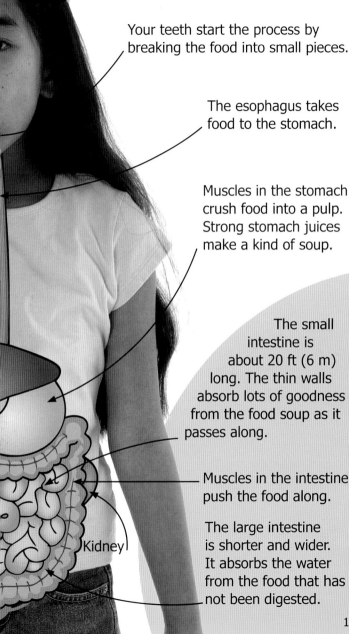

Your teeth start the process by breaking the food into small pieces.

The esophagus takes food to the stomach.

Muscles in the stomach crush food into a pulp. Strong stomach juices make a kind of soup.

The small intestine is about 20 ft (6 m) long. The thin walls absorb lots of goodness from the food soup as it passes along.

Muscles in the intestine push the food along.

The large intestine is shorter and wider. It absorbs the water from the food that has not been digested.

Kidney

15

Teeth

Young children grow a set of 20 milk teeth. When you are six or seven, these teeth gradually fall out and adult teeth grow in their place. The biggest molars are called wisdom teeth and may not break through until you are in your twenties. Adults have 32 teeth, 16 in each jaw.

As you grow, your jaw gets bigger, so that there is room for more teeth.

Remains of food and saliva form a sticky mixture called plaque. This attacks the enamel on your teeth and also your gums, so it is important to brush your teeth and gums after you have eaten.

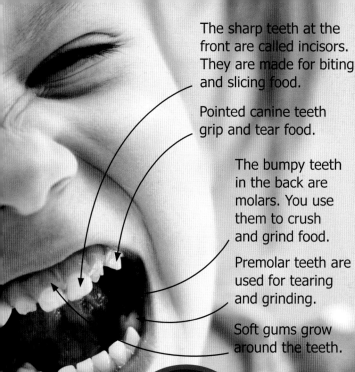

The sharp teeth at the front are called incisors. They are made for biting and slicing food.

Pointed canine teeth grip and tear food.

The bumpy teeth in the back are molars. You use them to crush and grind food.

Premolar teeth are used for tearing and grinding.

Soft gums grow around the teeth.

Inside a tooth

Crown

Gum

Enamel is the hard material that covers the tooth.

Under the enamel is a layer of dentine. This is tough and like a bone.

The middle of the tooth is soft. Nerves and blood vessels run through here.

Each tooth has its own root, which affixes it firmly in the jaw bone.

Smell and taste

Your senses of smell and taste work together, although your sense of smell is 20,000 times more sensitive than your sense of taste!

Your tongue, the roof of your mouth, and the back of your throat are all covered with taste buds.

Taste buds pick up sweet, sour, salty, and bitter flavors.

Your tongue also picks up the strong, savory flavor known as umami.

18

Your nose

To smell something, you breathe in air through your nose. Tiny, hairlike nerves in the top inside part of your nose sense chemicals in the air and send messages about the smell to your brain.

Tasty trick!

Try this to see how much your sense of smell affects what you taste! Block your nose. Can you taste the difference between a carrot and a cucumber?

19

Hearing and balance

Sounds are tiny vibrations in the air. When you hear, your ears pick up these vibrations and send signals along nerves to the brain. There are three main parts to the ear: the outer ear, the middle ear, and the inner ear.

Your outer ear collects sound vibrations and funnels them along the ear canal. The bones in your head also pass sounds through to your cochlea.

Ears for balance

Your inner ears also help you keep your balance. The semicircular canals are full of liquid. As you move, tiny hairs sense this liquid moving and send messages to the brain.

20

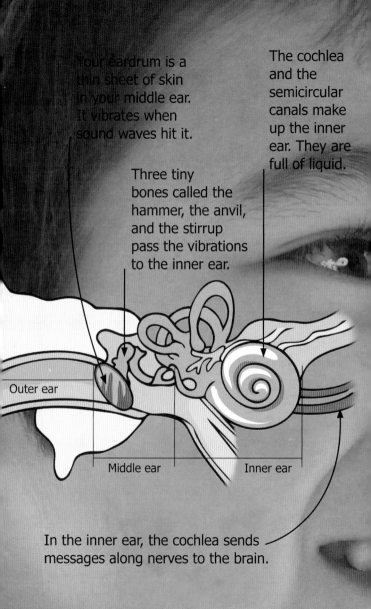

Your eardrum is a thin sheet of skin in your middle ear. It vibrates when sound waves hit it.

The cochlea and the semicircular canals make up the inner ear. They are full of liquid.

Three tiny bones called the hammer, the anvil, and the stirrup pass the vibrations to the inner ear.

Outer ear

Middle ear

Inner ear

In the inner ear, the cochlea sends messages along nerves to the brain.

21

Seeing

When light enters your eyes, nerve cells at the back of the eyes send messages to your brain. Your brain sorts the messages out so that you can see.

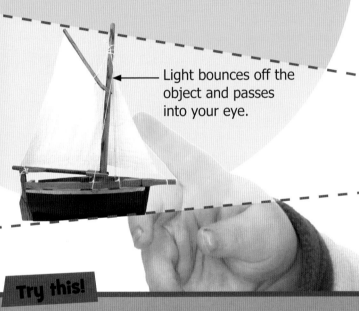

Light bounces off the object and passes into your eye.

Try this!

Your eyes are set apart, so each eye sees a slightly different picture and your brain puts them together. Try closing one eye and pointing at something. Keeping your finger still, look through the other eye. Are you pointing at the same thing?

The colored part of your eye is called the iris.

The optic nerve takes messages from the eye to your brain.

The black part of your eye, called the pupil, is in fact a hole. Light enters the eye here.

Cells on the retina make sense of light and color.

The lens bends the light.

The image on the retina is upside down.

Did you know?

Most people blink about 15 times a minute.

Touch

A huge network of nerve endings all over your body controls your sense of touch. Cells in the lower layer of the skin sense whether things you touch are hot, cold, soft, hard, rough, or smooth and send messages along nerves to your brain.

Nerve cells in the finger send a message to your spine. ⟶

The spine sends a message to the muscles in the arm, telling them to move the finger away.

When you prick your finger on a thorn, you pull your finger away very quickly.

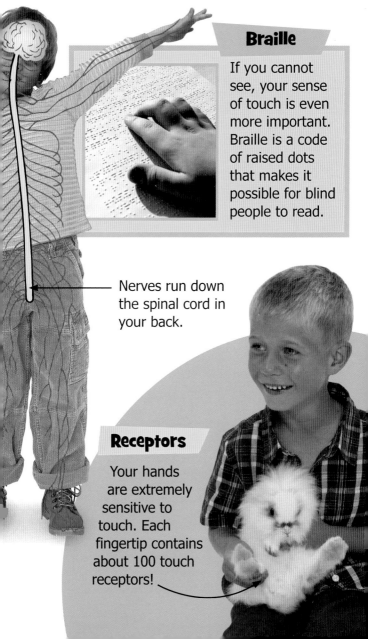

Braille

If you cannot see, your sense of touch is even more important. Braille is a code of raised dots that makes it possible for blind people to read.

Nerves run down the spinal cord in your back.

Receptors

Your hands are extremely sensitive to touch. Each fingertip contains about 100 touch receptors!

Skin

Your skin provides a waterproof, protective covering to your body. It can sense when things are hot or cold. If it gets cut, the skin will repair itself. Hairs grow on all parts of your skin, except for the soles of your feet, the palms of your hands, and your lips!

The outer layer of skin is known as the epidermis. The cells here are dead. They protect the lower layer.

The lower layer of skin is known as the dermis.

Sweat glands produce sweat to cool the skin down.

Blood vessels provide the skin with oxygen and food.

A layer of fat just under the skin helps to keep the body warm.

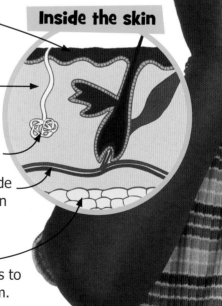

Inside the skin

26

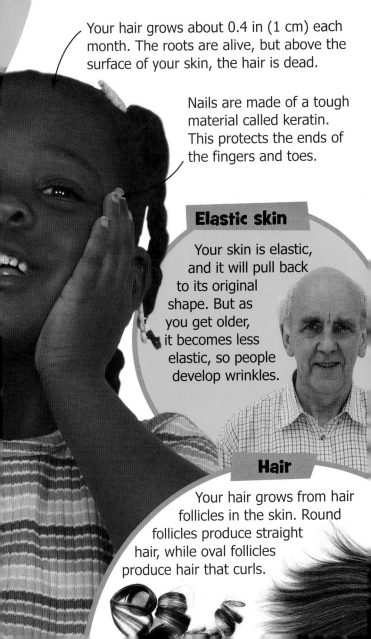

Your hair grows about 0.4 in (1 cm) each month. The roots are alive, but above the surface of your skin, the hair is dead.

Nails are made of a tough material called keratin. This protects the ends of the fingers and toes.

Elastic skin

Your skin is elastic, and it will pull back to its original shape. But as you get older, it becomes less elastic, so people develop wrinkles.

Hair

Your hair grows from hair follicles in the skin. Round follicles produce straight hair, while oval follicles produce hair that curls.

Brain power

Your brain is your body's control center. It makes it possible for you to think and move. You use your brain to speak, see, hear, touch, and taste things. It works all day and all night, even when you are asleep. Here are a small number of the things your brain can do.

The front of the brain is linked with personality.

Left or right?

In right-handed people, the left side of the brain is responsible for facts, figures, and language. The right side controls the ability to draw and make music. But for left-handed people, this may be reversed.

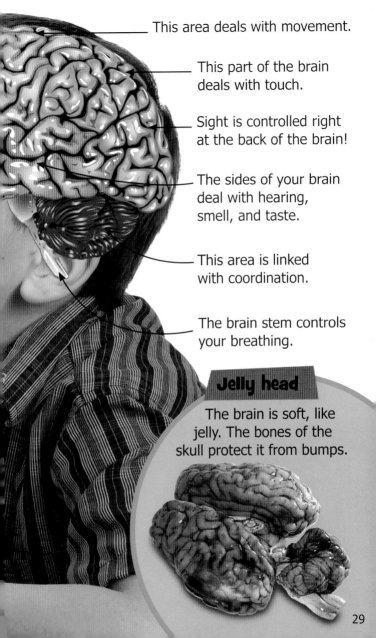

This area deals with movement.

This part of the brain deals with touch.

Sight is controlled right at the back of the brain!

The sides of your brain deal with hearing, smell, and taste.

This area is linked with coordination.

The brain stem controls your breathing.

Jelly head

The brain is soft, like jelly. The bones of the skull protect it from bumps.

Glossary

This glossary explains some of the harder words in the book.

artery A blood vessel carrying blood away from your heart.

balance When you balance, you stand in a steady position, without falling over.

blood The liquid that carries goodness and waste around your body.

bone marrow The soft, living tissue inside bones that makes new blood cells.

breathe When you breathe in, your chest expands and you take in air.

capillaries The very small blood vessels that form a network to carry blood throughout your body.

carbon dioxide A waste gas produced by your body. You breathe it out.

cochlea The part of the ear that looks like the shell of a snail. It converts sound vibrations into nerve messages to send to the brain.

germs Tiny living things that get into your body and can make you ill. Bacteria and viruses are germs.

lungs The part of the body that absorbs oxygen and gets rid of carbon dioxide.

muscle Strong, soft tissue that tightens or loosens in order to move parts of your body.

nerves Nerves carry messages between your brain and the rest of your body.

oxygen A gas that you breathe in. It is needed by all parts of your body.

retina A layer at the back of the eye that senses the light in the eye and sends messages to the brain.

ribs The structure of bones that protects the heart and lungs.

skeleton The strong framework of your body, made of more than 200 bones.

skull Formed from a number of bones that are joined together, the skull protects the brain.

stomach The bag that crushes food into a kind of soup.

tendons The tough bands that join muscle to a bone.

vein A blood vessel carrying blood towards your heart.

vibration When something vibrates, it makes small movements. Our ears hear the vibrations of the air as different sounds.

vocal cords The flaps of tissue that vibrate when you talk or sing.

voice box The part of your body that contains your vocal cords and makes it possible for you to speak and sing.